Human Movement

Nicolas Brasch

Australia • Brazil • Japan • Korea • Mexico • Singapore • Spain • United Kingdom • United States

Human Movement

Fast Forward
Blue Level 11

Text: Nicolas Brasch
Editor: Kate McGough
Design: Vonda Pestana
Series design: James Lowe
Production controller: Emma Hayes
Photo research: Corrina Tauschke
Audio recordings: Juliet Hill, Picture Start
Spoken by: Matthew King and Abbe Holmes
Reprint: Jennifer Foo

Acknowledgements
The author and publisher would like to acknowledge permission to reproduce material from the following sources: Photographs by APL/Corbis/Jolanda Cats & Hans Withoos/Zefa, cover, pp 1, 13 bottom left; Getty Images/Gallo Images/Shaen Adey, p 9 top; istockphoto.com, p 4 top/ Laura Fisher, p 12 bottom left/ Denise McQuillen, p 5 top; Lindsay Edwards, p 13 top right; Masterfile/J D Heaton, p 9 bottom; Newsphotos.com, p 11 bottom/ John Appleyard, p 7 bottom/ Tom Campbell, p 5 bottom/ Mark Frecker, p 8 right; Photolibrary.com/Aflo Foto Agency, back cover, pp 3, 6 bottom, 15 bottom; Photolibrary.com/Index Stock Imagery, pp 7 top, 10 centre/ Photonica Inc, p 12 top; Photos.com, pp 4 bottom, 10 bottom left, 14 left, 15 top/ Photolibrary.com/Age Fotostock/Alain Evrard, p 8 left/ Dennis MacDonald, p 6 top/ Super Stock, p 11 top/ Photolibrary.com/Science Photo Library/Alfred Pasieka, p 14 right.

ISBN 978 0 17 012558 1
ISBN 978 0 17 012549 9 (set)

Cengage Learning Australia
Level 7, 80 Dorcas Street
South Melbourne, Victoria Australia 3205
Phone: 1300 790 853

Cengage Learning New Zealand
Unit 4B Rosedale Office Park
331 Rosedale Road, Albany, North Shore NZ 0632
Phone: 0508 635 766

For learning solutions, visit cengage.com.au

Printed in Australia by Ligare Pty Ltd
6 7 8 9 10 11 12 21 20 19 18 17

THE UNIVERSITY OF MELBOURNE

Evaluated in independent research by staff from the Department of Language, Literacy and Arts Education at the University of Melbourne.

Human Movement

Nicolas Brasch

Contents

Chapter 1

MOVEMENT

Fish can swim.

Most birds can fly and walk.

Dogs can walk, run and roll.

Humans can move in lots of ways, too.

Chapter 2

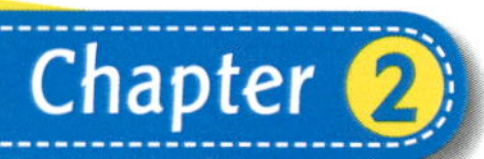

MOVEMENT IN SPORT

Humans move in different ways for sport.

In some sports, people jump high into the air.

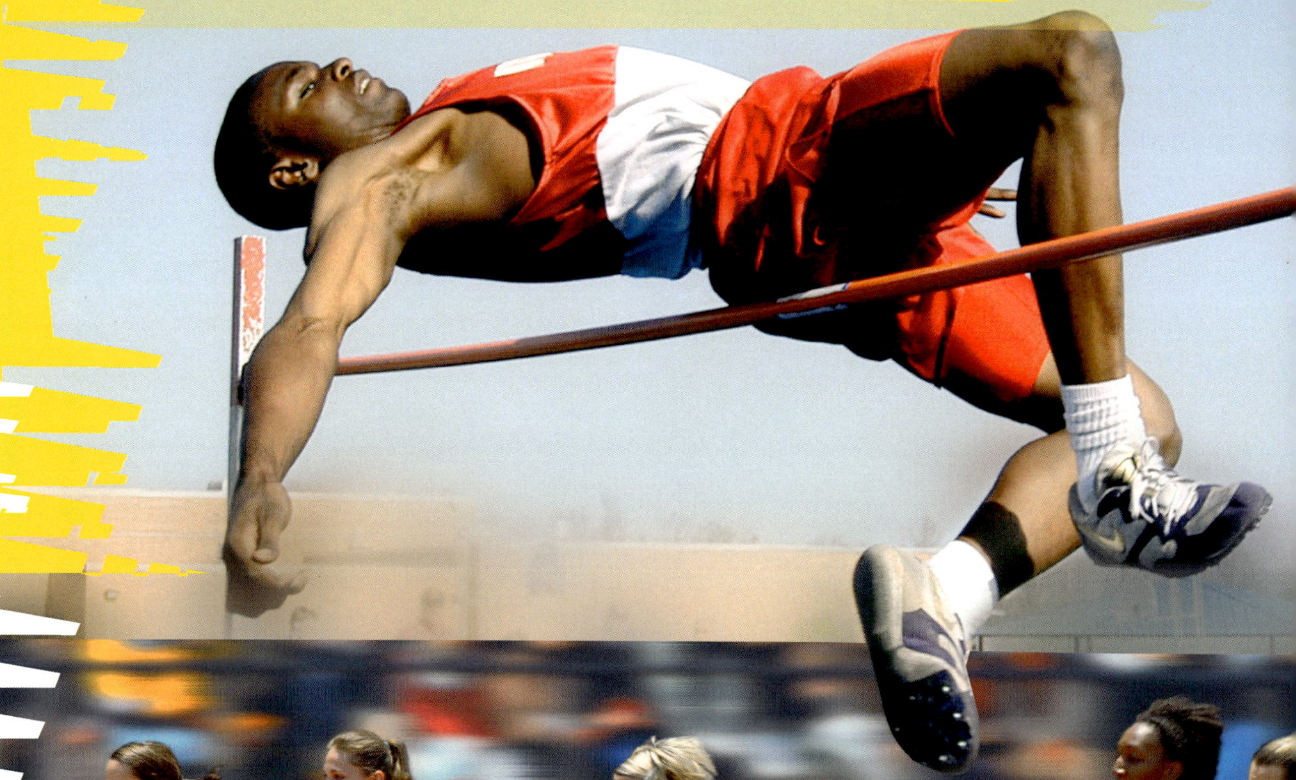

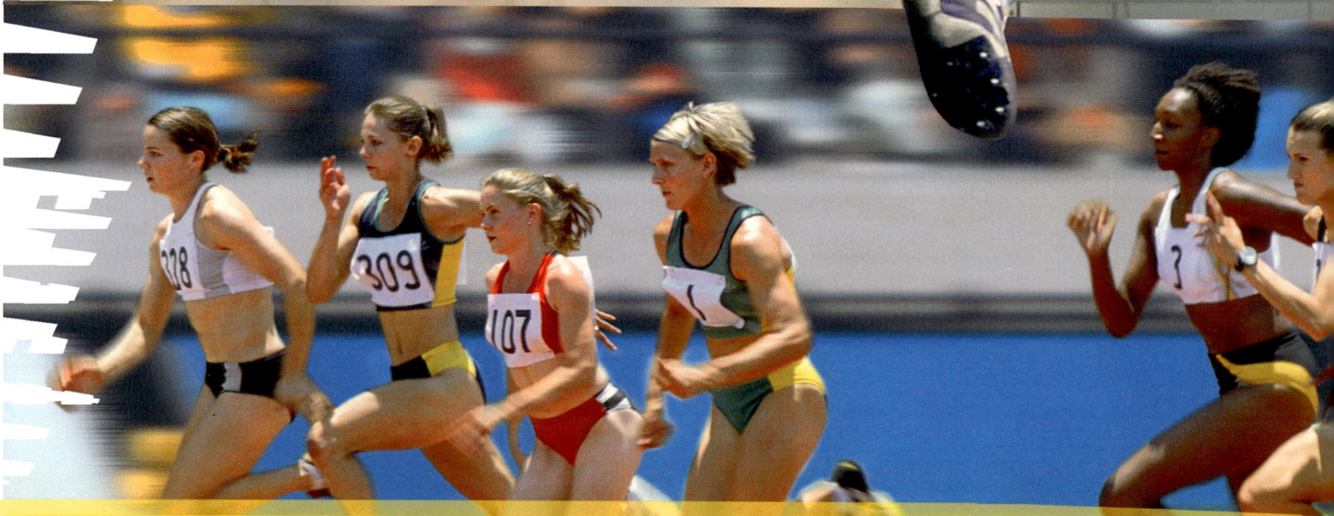

In some sports, people run as fast as they can.

In some sports, people turn upside down and dive into water.

In some sports, people move their arms so they can throw and catch a ball.

Chapter 3

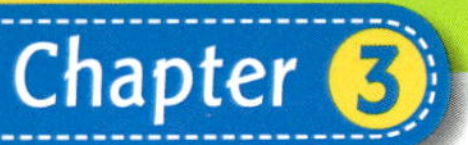

MOVEMENT IN THE ARTS

Humans move in different ways in the **arts**.

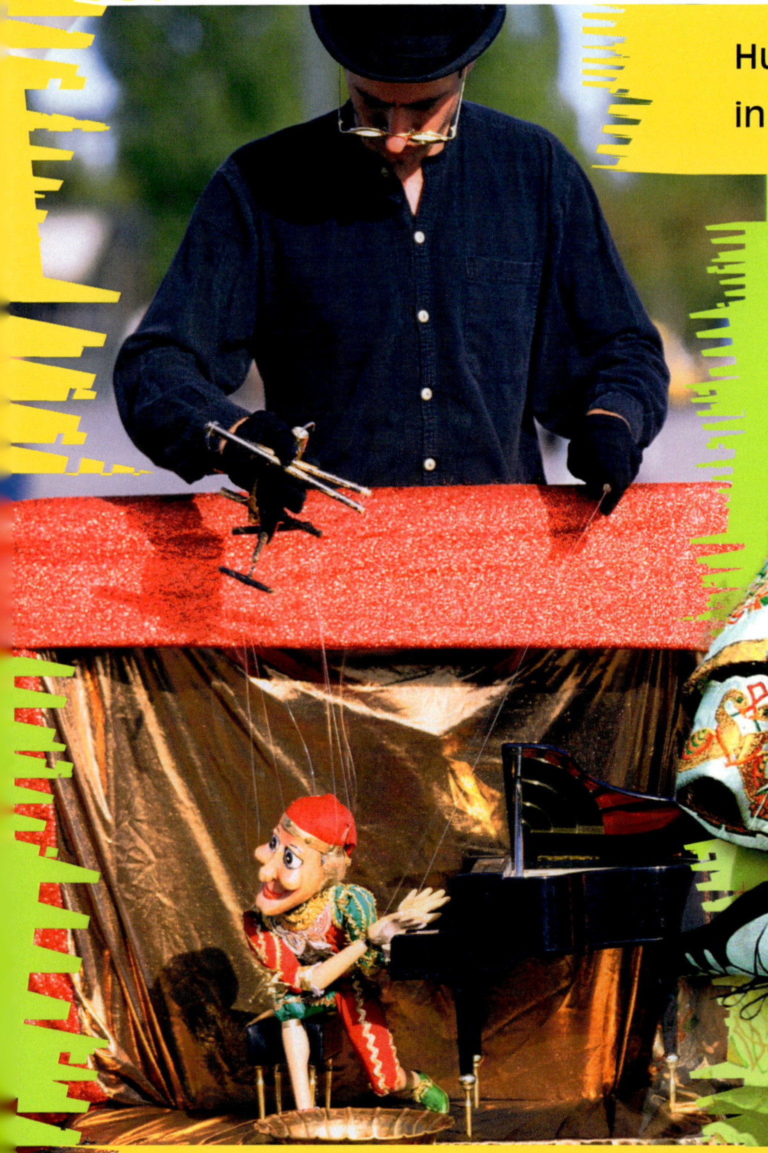

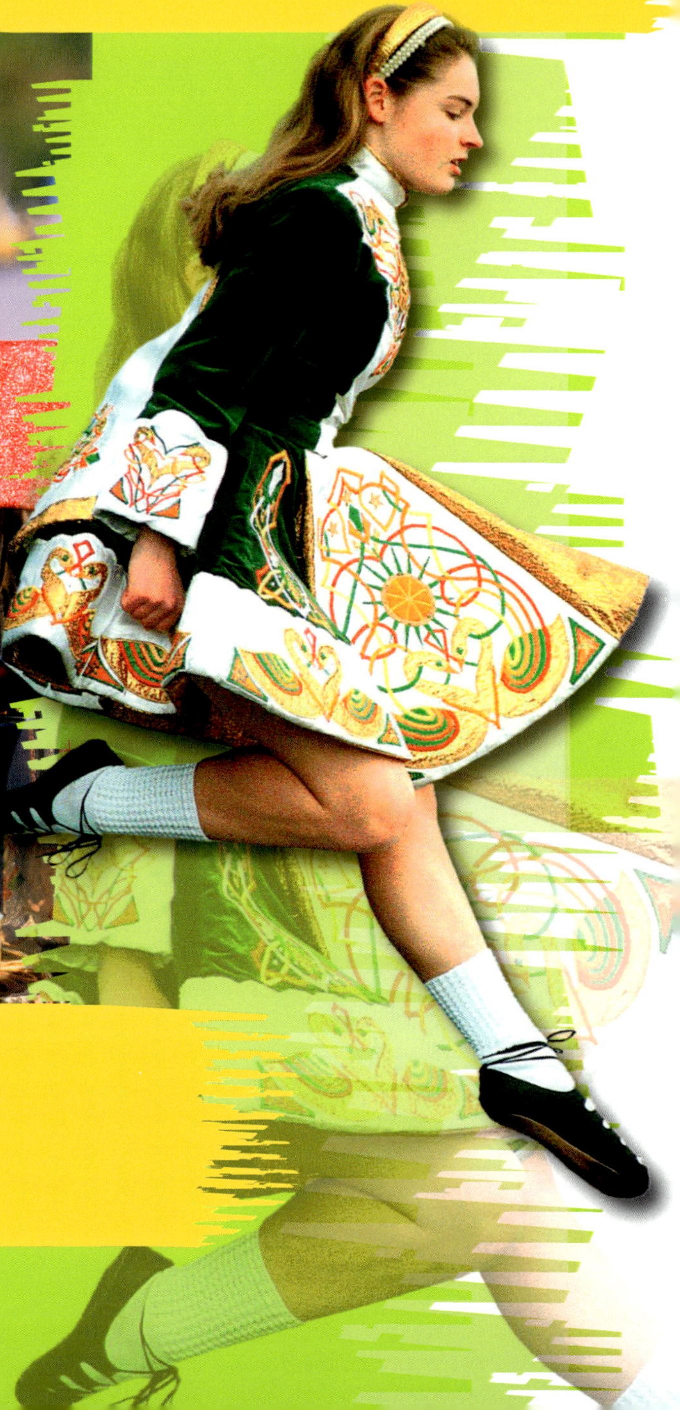

Some artists move their arms and hands.

Some artists move their legs.

Some artists move their mouths and fingers.

Some artists move different parts of their **bodies** at the same time.

Running Words 114

MOVEMENT AT WORK

Humans move in different ways at work.

Some people move their arms and hands at work. If they didn't, cars would hit each other.

Some people move their fingers at work so that their work gets done.

Running Words 151

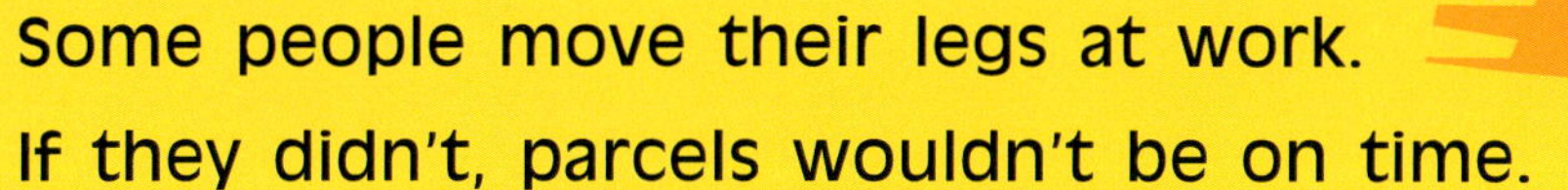

Some people move their legs at work.
If they didn't, parcels wouldn't be on time.

Some people move their eyes at work
so that they don't miss any action.

Chapter 5

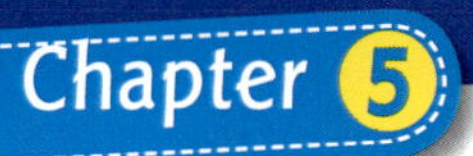

MOVEMENT FOR FUN

Humans also move in different ways to have fun.

Some people move their legs when having fun, so they can jump into the air.

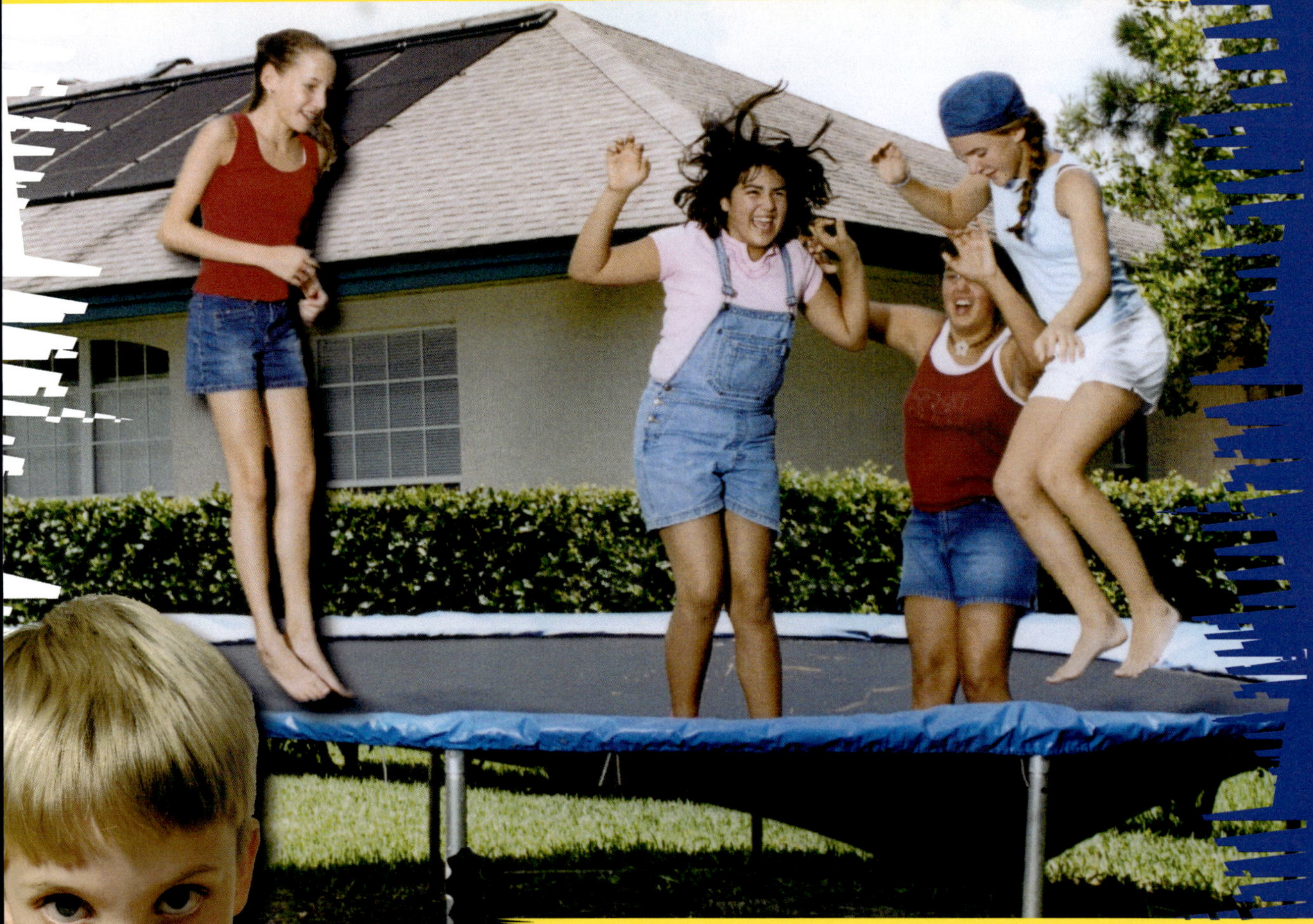

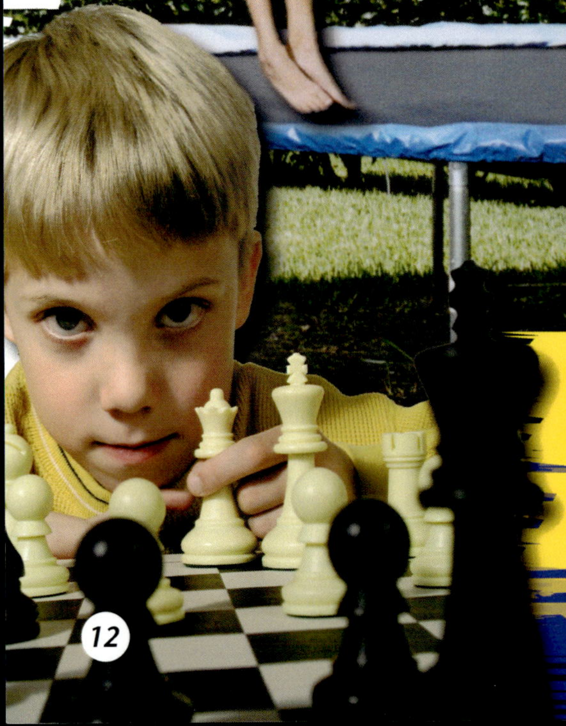

Some people move their fingers when having fun, so they can make the right moves.

Some people move their eyes when having fun, so they don't miss any action.

Some people move everything when having fun.

MOVEMENT WHILE RESTING

When humans are resting,
their bodies do not stay still.

People's eyes move when they are reading.

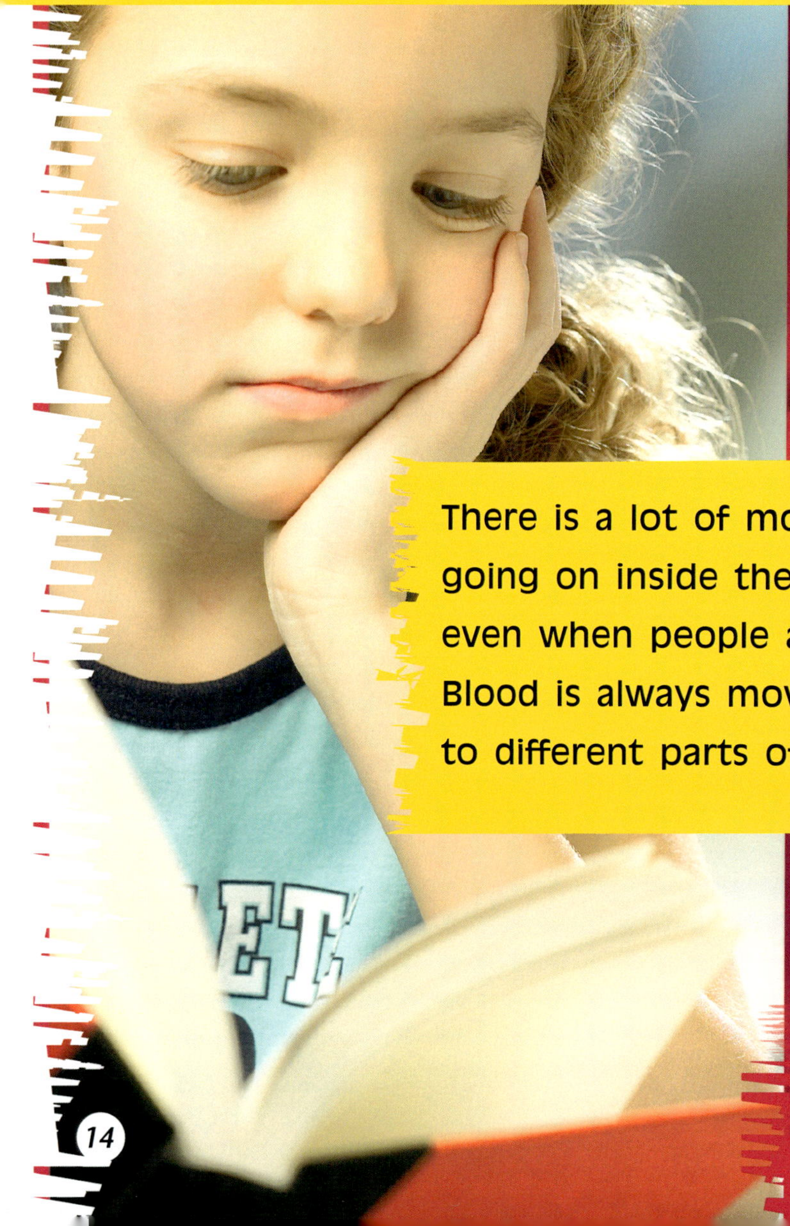

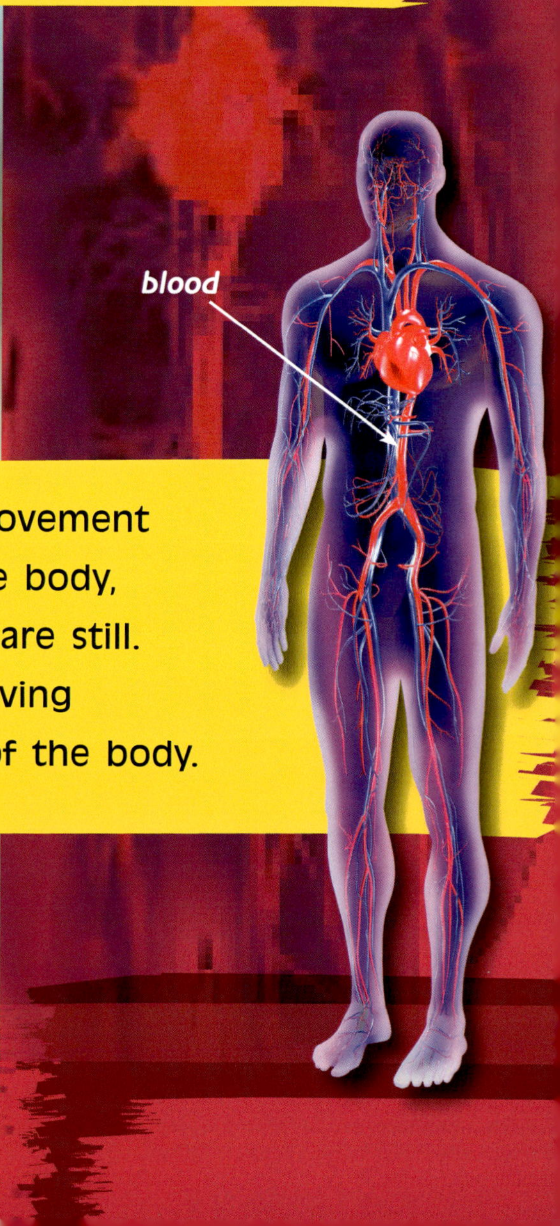

There is a lot of movement going on inside the body, even when people are still. Blood is always moving to different parts of the body.

blood

The human body never stops moving.

Glossary

arts a creative activity such as music, dance or painting

body the bones, flesh and organs of a person or animal

Index